# Sights through Poetry

## Volume I

Aliyah Rana'

For information, contact soul_child266@hotmail.com.

Cover Photography: Aliyah Rana' Sims

ISBN 978-0-9842684-2-9

# CONTENTS

# INTRODUCTION

When I was a little girl, I would often stare into a mirror and wonder "What am I here for?" I've been writing here and there all my life, but it wasn't until I signed up for a poetry course my junior year of college that I began to *really* write. Throughout the course, I received praises both in and out of the classroom for my writing. It wasn't the positive feedback that made me want to pursue a career as a writer; it was the realization that what I wrote actually affected people. I consider this collection the first seed in a career that will include more collections, songs, and (perhaps) books. As my father puts it, "A writer writes!"

## Mr. Man

Soft brown skin.
Round bald head.
Warm brown eyes.

Feathers and beads adorned your sleek
leather vest as single feather rose above
your tall frame from your headdress.

Naked skin peeked between the
curtain-like space created
by your vest's
opening.

That store.
As gray as the sidewalk it lined.
Old items on old shelves waiting for
their next owners.

I gave you small grins and thankful
eyes every time you gave me a toy.

It's funny how I don't remember
much about Jersey.

But I do remember you.

# Sunday Mornings

Hallelujahs sprout from
mouths accompanying
the rhythm of stomping
on rickety hard wood.

Round ladies fan faces
shaded by well-brimmed
hats and rock from side
to side on heavy-cushioned
bottoms.

Voice loud like thunder
cracks silence like
lightning while sweat
rolls down stressed face.
Soft dividing creases of
a loose robe are disrupted
by quick, curt movements.

Mouth is interrupted by
a cycle of words and
napkin wipes like
clockwork.

### His Life, Perhaps.


Young boy.
Breathless yells of play
escape as feet
seemingly flow
above greens and browns.


Young man.
Yells of laughter
jolt ears as his
head leans back
to release chasing
chuckles.


Old man.
Lying in room as
yells of nothingness
fill sterile halls.

# Home Now

Shiny linoleum floors
mirror lives that
reverse in memory
as the standstill of
time draws near.

Figures draped in
Flesh stagger about
as the scent of
piss and death
wavers around
scrunched noses.

Eyes glazed in gray
wildly wander
through time long gone
as lips release
jumbled thinking.

# The Way She Used to Be

I remember watching her
stitch up old clothes.
Eyes looking below glasses
as weathered hands flip and
turn the needle throughout  fabric.
On a clear day, she would wheel
clothes outside and put them
into a basket in the storage room.
She never bothered to properly
wear her old loafers.
She'd just slide her feet inside
the shoes as if they were flip flops.
This was wash day.
She always had a peaceful look
on her face as she listened
to the clothes turn about
in the washing machine.
The bordered patches created
by her face's deep crevices would
sag as she looked out into the
blossoming garden like a captain
gazing at the infinite sea.
Now she limps.

## Depths

I sit as you tease sand
and my tip toes.  Both dark
like cocoa hue of
coconuts' thick crust.


The moon pulls you away
as feet  search for  grained earth.
Eyes see endlessly deep
as returned soil brings truth.

# City Life

Bright lights
Tall buildings
Live music
Loud laughter

Dark streets
Shambled buildings
Silent corners
Distant talking

Only a few blocks away.

## Haiti, USA

Dust covers skin
blackened by sun
and dirt.

Mangled bodies line
crumbled crumbling
streets.

Cries of sorrow fill
ears as the scent of
decaying bodies fill
noses like water
pouring from
broken levees.

## Kelton

Dirt roads pave the way.
Shack slanted sideways
fills with Black faces
every Friday night.

Aged smiles seep out as
brown lips with pink paths
burnt by gin stretch wide
to cuss and to laugh.

Gladness fills corners
as Al Green fills ears.
Children play and watch,
and wait 'til their turn.

## Paper Snowflakes

Laughing, whispering
frolicking voices
fill a small room
with tiled ceilings
and cold floors
scattered with clipped
paper.

Tiny feet skip
as bangs and braids
wisp. Toothless smiles
release tumbling
giggles that mask
thoughts of home. '

# Vicky

She was thirteen.
Only a child.
Younger in mind.
Older in flesh.

She was funny
with a vulgar
sense of humor.
Life was in her.

Her hair hung thick
like the soft flow
of water from
a pitcher's mouth.

She is nineteen.
Four small children.
She is funny.
She still has that.

## For Derrion Albert

Red blood from Black
body covers grey
pavement like clear
puddles after a rainy day.

Shouts of fear surround
a scattered crowd as
hurried sounds of
shoe bottoms
meeting street tops
supply the chaos.

Yells of sadness try
to reverse time as the
camera keeps rolling.

## ABOUT THE AUTHOR

Aliyah Rana' was born in Jersey City, New Jersey in August of 1989. She was raised in the small, rural town of Jonesville, South Carolina.  There she lived mostly with her grandmother, mother, and uncle. After her freshman year of high school, Aliyah moved to Rock Hill, South Carolina, where her mother and father remarried. While completing her high school career in Rock Hill, she discovered her liking for writing when she inadvertently enrolled in a journalism course. She eventually became the editorial editor for the school's newspaper. After high school she entered Winthrop University as a journalism major. She later changed her major to English as her interest in creative writing grew. At Winthrop, she discovered her natural talent for writing poetry while completing a poetry course. She is currently a senior at Winthrop University and spends her free time writing poetry and songs.

**Aliyah Rana' can be contacted by email at:**

**soul_child266@hotmail.com**

www.ingramcontent.com/pod-product-compliance
Lightning Source LLC
Chambersburg PA
CBHW030304030426
42337CB00012B/580